SYSTEMOLOGY
PROCEDURES

POCKET EDITION

Published from
Mardukite Borsippa HQ, San Luis Valley, Colorado
Mardukite Academy & Systemology Society
for spiritual or philosophical purposes only

SYSTEMOLOGY PROCEDURES

ADVANCED SKILLS IN PROCESSING

Advanced Training Supplement
developed by Joshua Free for
the Systemology Society

THE JOSHUA FREE IMPRINT
JFI PUBLICATIONS

ISBN : 978-1-961509-46-7

This manual is restricted to students using:
The Systemology Professional Course -or-
The Advanced Training Course

Full use of this book also requires the
"Systemology Biofeedback"
Advanced Training Supplement

Based on a lecture series by Joshua Free
given during the 2023 Winter Solstice

First Edition Pocket Paperback — *February 2024*

mardukite.com

Take Systemology To New Levels!

The Official Mardukite Systemology "Procedure Manual" is now available to the public for the very first time.

Seekers working on the "Pathway to Ascension" using the Systemology "Professional Course" and "Advanced Training Course" can learn how to more effectively apply Systemology techniques to reach even more advanced levels of spiritual clearing.

This manual concisely organizes the most critical information necessary to expertly Co-Pilot and Solo-Pilot. The "hows" and "whys" of our methods are laid out clearly for all Seekers to understand and powerfully use.

Never before has Joshua Free so concisely demonstrated the theory and practice of this spiritual technology. Master the art of defragmenting "energetic turbulence" and overcome the "spiritual implants" introduced in the Professional Course and A.T. materials, which keep us bound to this Universe!

"Keys to the Kingdom"
Official Advanced Training Course
Series Coming Soon!

TABLET OF CONTENTS

INTRODUCTION TO
THE MANUAL

This manual is restricted to students using:
The Systemology Professional Course -or-
The Advanced Training Course

Full use of this manual also requires:
"Systemology Biofeedback"

INTRODUCING THE SYSTEMOLOGY PROCEDURES MANUAL

Mardukite Systemology is a new evolution in Human understanding about the "systems" governing *Life*, *Reality*, the *Universe* and all *Existences*. It is also a *Spiritual Path* used to transcend the Human experience and reach *"Ascension."*

This is an advanced professional course supplement (manual) detailing how to *apply* physical technology to our spiritual philosophy to enhance a *Seeker's* personal progress on the *"Pathway"* to Ascension.

This manual supplements our *Professional Course* series of lessons—available as individual booklets, or collected in two volumes titled *"The Pathway to Ascension"* The *Professional Course* follows after material given in the *Basic Course* booklets, or *"Fundamentals of Systemology"* volume.

The systematic methodology that we use to assist an individual to increase their *"Actualized Awareness"* (and reach gradually higher toward their *"Spiritual Ascension"*) is referred to as *"The Pathway"* — and that individual is called a *"Seeker."*

To receive the greatest benefit from this manual: it is expected that a *Seeker* will already be familiar with the fundamental concepts and terminology (previously relayed in the *Basic Course* and *Professional Course* lessons) of our *applied philosophy.*

As a *Seeker* increases their *Awareness* in this lifetime, their spiritual *"Knowingness"* also increases—which is to say their *certainty* on *Life*, on this and other *Universes*, and on *realizing Self* as an unlimited "spiritual being" *having* an enforced restrictive "human experience." A *Seeker* also *knowingly* increases their command and control of the "human experience." And this is a part of what is meant by *"Actualized Awareness."*

THREE STATES OF KNOWINGNESS

Raising a *Seeker's* level of *Actualized Awareness* requires, by definition, "bringing what is *hidden* (or not consciously known) up into the realm of *light* or *Knowingness.*" We might go as far to say, as an imperfect example, that there are three primary states of *Knowingness*: *actual knowing*, *almost knowing* and *not-knowing*.

Actual knowing is what an individual is conscious of and can easily recall as needed. It makes up our "surface" (or "above-the-surface") thoughts; what is *"actually known"* and available to *Self* for "inspection" or analytical thought. This includes what we have *certainty* on as part of our *reality*.

Then, there are other *things* "below-the-surface" that we do not easily remember

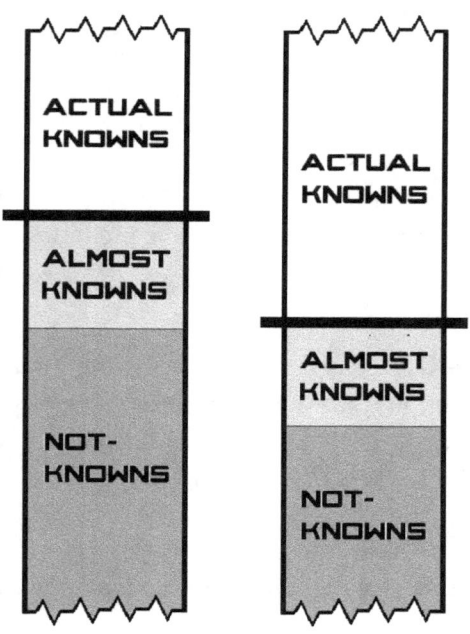

14

(or have any *reality* on)—and these fit our other categories of *almost knowing* and *not-knowing*. One key difference between these other two states is how *far* "below-the-surface" a *thing* is.

What you "*almost know*" are those *things* just "below-the-surface"—so *close* to the "surface" that they are almost accessible. This "gray area" includes what an individual is *uncertain* of. With a little assistance ("*Systematic Processing*" techniques), you can actually move a *thing* that is "*almost known*" to an "above-the-surface" state of "*actually knowing*" or remembering again. Only then may it be treated with any *certainty*.

There are also memories very deeply buried "below-the-surface." This includes suppressed data that is not currently accessible—and therefore, presently "*not-known*." Once again, there is a way to move *things* from this state into another state. For this to happen, the previous *"almost known" things* ("just-below-the-surface") need to be "purged" (at least partially) by *"resurfacing"* them into *"actually known" things*.

As more layers of *"almost knowns"* are *resurfaced* into *"actual knowns,"* more of what is *"not-known"* becomes accessible within the "gray area." *Systematic Processing* techniques of *Systemology* are intended to target this "gray area" — promoting increased *realizations* by elevating more *knowledge* and *present-time attention* to a state of *Actual Awareness*.

What is already *"known"* is easily accessed with *systematic processing*. When using *Biofeedback* technology, we are most interested in the *"almost knowns,"* This area is accessible with *Biofeedback* even when a *Seeker* is not yet fully *aware* of it. But, more deeply buried *"not-knowns"* are still not accessible until more layers come off and they become *"almost knowns."*

CHARTING FLIGHTS ON THE PATHWAY

Although there is a systematic structure to *fragmentation*, the personal journey experienced along the *Pathway* will be different for each *Seeker*. For example, certain areas will seem more "*turbulent*" or difficult for one *Seeker* than another. We tend to say that these areas have more "*charge*" on them—or that they are more "*heavily charged.*" It is best to handle such areas when you are already feeling "good" and not in a situation (or condition) where that specific area is consistently being "*triggered*" or "*restimulated.*"

As an applied philosophy, *Systemology* "theory" can be easily utilized in the "laboratory" of the "world-at-large" in everyday life. This is implied within the basic instruction of each lesson. Unlike other "sciences" that conduct experiments by making a change to some "objective variable" *out there* and waiting to see an effect, our focus is the individual (or *Observer*) themselves, and how *they* affect the *"Reality"* perceived.

Our philosophy is applied by using specific exercises and systematic techniques. These *"processes"* provide the most stable personal gain (and *realizations*) for each area; but only when actually applied with a *Seeker's* full *"presence"* and *Awareness*. Hundreds of such *processes* may be found in the *"Pathway to Ascension"* (*Professional Course*) material.

Applying a technique is called *"running a process."* *Processes* are designed with very simple instructions or *"command-lines."* To *run* a *processing command-line*, a *Seeker* may be assisted by the communication of that *line* from a *"Co-Pilot"* (as in *"Traditional Piloting"*). But even then, a *Seeker* must still personally *"input"* the *command* as *Self*. For this reason—and quite thankfully—*Solo-Processing* is possible.

TAKING FLIGHT ON THE PATHWAY

Processing Techniques are intended to treat the *Spiritual Being* or *Alpha-Spirit*; the individual themselves. The *"command-lines"* are *directed to* the individual themselves—not some *mental machinery* of theirs, and not even a *Biofeedback* metering device.

Systematic Processing is applied by the *Alpha-Spirit*—who then *Self-directs* command of their "Mind-System" or "body" (*genetic-vehicle*), both of which are "constructs" that the *Alpha-Spirit* (*Self*, or the "I-AM" *Awareness unit*) operates, but neither of which is actually *Self*. *Fragmentation* causes *Humans* to falsely identify *Self as* the *"Mind"* or even a *"Body."*

Some *processes* can be treated quite lightly at first; others may require a bit of working at in order to get *"running"* well. It is important to set aside a period of time when you can be dedicated to your studies and *processing*. This period of time is referred to as a *"processing session."* When a *process* does start *running* well, it is important to be able to complete it to a satisfactory *"end-point."*

Processing allows us to be able to *actually* "look" at *things* and even determine the *considerations* we have made—or attitudes we have decided—about *Reality* as a result of those experiences.

It doesn't do us much good to simply "glance"—or to *restimulate* something uncomfortable and then quickly *withdraw* from it once again, leaving more of our *attention* yet again behind and held fixedly on it.

Generally speaking, a *Seeker* continues to *run* a *process* so long as something is "happening"—which is to say, the *process* is still producing a change. Usually this is evident by the type of "answers" that a *command-line* prompts a *Seeker* to originate from the database of their own *Mind-System*.

Processing Command-Lines ("PCL") are not "magic words"; they do not "do" anything on their own. They systematically assist a *Seeker* to direct their own attention toward increasing *Awareness*.

A *Seeker* may also cease to generate new "data" from a *process* without reaching an *"ultimate" realization* as an *"end-point."* It is possible that additional "layers" (or even other "areas") require handling before anything "deeper" is accessible. If this is the case, end the *process*. But, if a *Seeker* is *withdrawing* from something uncomfortable that was incited or stirred up, then a *process* is *run* until they feel "good" about it.

One of the benefits to *Flying-Solo* on the *Pathway* is that the *processing* is entirely *Self-determined.* This naturally provides a certain built-in "safety" for a practitioner. Anything you *restimulate* by *Self-determinism* is *your thing*. It is not triggered or incited by some external *"other-determined"* influences (or other "source-points" in existence) that make you an *effect*. It can be more easily handled in *processing*—or you can simply let things "cool down" and come back to it again in another *session*.

While it may seem "mysterious" to beginners, a *Seeker* gets a sense for knowing how long to *run* a *process* only with practice.

Once you have spent some time actually applying material from *"The Pathway to Ascension" Professional Course*, there are many aspects of it that become "second nature" because they are, in fact, a part of our true original native nature. All we have done in *Systemology* is *"reverse engineer"* the routes of *creation* and *consideration* that are already *our own*.

SYSTEMOLOGY PROCEDURES (THE MANUAL)

"MANY YEARS AGO, I REALIZED
THAT 'THE WAY OUT' WOULD
SYSTEMATICALLY RESEMBLE
THE ROUTES BY WHICH WE
ORIGINALLY DESCENDED."
—*Joshua Free*
Backtrack Lectures

SYSTEMATIC PROCESSING
& THE ALPHA-SPIRIT

Fragmentation occurs due to our desire to *create* (or *copy*) and *experience* "*everything*." In our native state, as a *god-like being*, this amounts to little more than watching a thrilling movie every once and a while to keep some of the more desirable conditions of existence '*fresh*'. We are, after all, quite *eternal*, and *boredom* is always a *fear*. But, this does not mean that the *effects* of these *creations* must *persist* and go on to perpetuate as *fragmentation* thereafter.

Actualized individuals are able to shake off *effects* of *fragmentation* like water. This is the ability a *Seeker* ultimately improves on the *Pathway*. The existence—and our continuous *unknowing creation*—of *fragmentation* is a quite unfortunate mistake we all have picked up quite early on our *Spiritual Timeline* and tracked along with us ever since.

Spiritual implanting (taking place long before the existence of *this Physical Universe*) misled us to believing that *thinking about, perceiving, experiencing* and/or *creating* certain "things" could actually permanently harm us. This resulted in us "*flinching*" or "*withdrawing*" from "things" for the very first time. Later, those same things were used to discourage and restrict our *thinking about, looking at, doing* and even *being* things—and now, we have found our *spiritual perception* quite *darkened*, and our *spiritual abilities* quite *fragmented*.

We exist as a *Potential Everythingness* that is balancing an *Infinity-of-Nothingness*; we never seem to allow ourselves to be rid of anything unless we have a *certainty* that we can *create* (*have*) it again in the future.

To "*lose*" anything permanently—even if only a *created mental image picture*—would be to take away (or reduce) the full quality of richness inherent in *Everythingness*.

This also means that an individual will not 'uncreate' any of their *continuously created* "things" unless they can *look at* a "thing" so clearly and completely *"As-It-Is,"* that they could *create (have)* it again.

The 'things' of *fragmentation unknowingly persist* because we believe that we should not *look at* them, and certainly not *create* them *knowingly* so as to have *responsibility* for their *creation*. When we *create "mental image" facsimile-copies* in our *processing exercises*, we demonstrate to an individual that they are capable of *recreating* at *will*. When we treat the *copy "As-It-Is,"* we also demonstrate they have abilities to make it "go away" or "disappear" too. Hence, when we bring something up "into view" during *systematic processing*, we are, at the very least, able to 'desensitize' some of the *fragmentation effects* using our *Awareness*.

The *willingness* to *create* something is also governed by the *willingness* to be *responsible* for the existence of a thing—and the effects that it *creates*. True *power* and *control* is only found in *full responsibility*. It also requires having *clear communication* and *perception*. These are all areas that a *Seeker* will target and improve upon with *systematic processing* on the *Pathway*.

Another part of *processing* is "*loosening of fixed considerations*." We are "reactively" inclined to not *like* 'things' that are "bad" —or two things in "conflict" with one another. We may even think "changing our mind" about a thing is a betrayal. Yet to be rid of any "bad" conditions, we must first decide to "*like*" it enough to *confront* it "*As-It-Is*." We must be able to at least *tolerate* it enough, have it *close* enough (for our *perception*), even for a moment, in order to *look at* it. We don't have to *have* it again; but we must be *willing* to *recreate* it in order for it to truly cease to *persist*.

Our methods represent the *systematic* opposite of how things are handled in a "human society" where things are continuously *suppressed* and buried out of view —which makes certain that the *fragmentation* goes on being *compulsively created unknowingly* out of our *control*.

Procedures and techniques for *systematic defragmentation* require skill and practice to be effective. The *"Pathway to Ascension" Professional Course* was designed with the *"Solo-Pilot"* in mind—though our original *Systemology Core* volumes (collecting the research and development) emphasized what is now called *"Traditional Piloting"* (where a trained professional "guides" a *Seeker* along the *Pathway*).

"Traditional Piloting" is not an option for *Systemology Level-7* and above. Even if a *Seeker* is *"Co-Piloted"* through earlier *processing-levels*: to continue with *"Advanced Training"* requires they study the *"Professional Course"* on their own—in addition to these *"Advanced Training Supplements"* —before using the *"Keys to the Kingdom" Advanced Training Course* as a *Solo-Pilot*.

Ideally, a *Seeker* will learn skills and gain the *certainty* necessary to apply *systematic processing* "as" *Self*, "to" *Self*. In the end, this is the only truly workable and effective method of "*setting one's Self free.*"

A "*free being*" that is not bound to a *Body* must also not be entirely reliant on "*biofeedback devices*" in order to maintain their *freedom* later on. However, to ensure we get there (relatively quickly)—and to learn how it is even possible—"*biofeedback technology*" is a critical tool applied to some *upper-level* procedures found in the "*Advanced Training Course.*" Basic details are given in the "*Systemology Biofeedback*" *Advanced Training Supplement*. Additional details are given in various course books.

The theory behind our approach is that: what an individual *actually knows* and/or is *knowingly creating*, is not the source of their *fragmentation*. But, in our present condition, if we *could* intuitively and instinctively *defragment* ourselves without the right training and use of technology, then we would have been *"out of here"* already. Of course, we've swallowed a lot of *false data* early in our existence, and this set the foundations—and *platforms*—for our being *fragmented.* Unfortunately, this is what causes our *"instinct"* to often lead us away from the upward *Pathway.*

A *Biofeedback "device"* is not described in the *"Professional Course"* materials, so that a *Seeker does* get practice handling our methods *"intuitively"* without it. This experience could be applied to *upper-levels*, approaching them without a *"device,"* but the progress is likely to be much slower.

SYSTEMATIC PROCEDURES

Systematic Processing is primarily *looking* and *seeing "What Is"*—As-It-Is. *"Processing Command Lines"* (or *"PCL"*) are really a query-line (or question) of *"what is"*? The response is based on whatever our *attention* (*Awareness*) is on, or directed to. Even when not worded as a literal question, a PCL is still a prompt for such a response. For example:

Q: *Recall a time when... (What is it?)*

A: *(It is) when such-and-such...*

Q: *Spot something in the... (What is it?)*

A: *(It is) that thing...*

Q: *Notice something about... (What is it?)*

A: *(It is) this...*

A *Seeker* is still permitted to *consider* or *wonder about* things. But to avoid having progress slow down to a halt during a *processing session*: the focus should be on what they *can identify, see,* or *know about,* rather than concentrating on "*unknowns.*" We can *consider* things we do not yet have a *Knowingness* of, but usually the solution is to work from a stable point, which rests on what we *do know* with *actual certainty.*

Systematic Processing also involves *"spotting"* What-Is *"repeatedly."* The best gains in *perception* occur when something is first *looked at.* Just watching it thereafter does not produce nearly as much change in *perception* for the amount of time spent doing so. Therefore, *attention* is often alternated "on" and "off" of something in order to *see* it more *clearly.* Or, you can shift *attention* onto different parts of large objects or a significant *"incident"* (rather than simply "stare" at it).

Some basic *processes* practice intentionally *reaching* and *withdrawing*; on a "physical" level, and with *attention.* When an area is *fragmented*, a *Seeker's attention* is either fixedly "stuck" *on* it, or else they have a "mental flinch" *away* from it (and are unlikely to *look* at all). To *defragment*, we *systematically* put *attention* "onto" and "off" of it—*knowingly* and *intentionally*—in order to restore ability to clearly and *Self-Honestly* think about and/or handle something.

There are times an individual might get away with applying *"fixed concentration"* to something—but it is usually the "long way" to get results. There is also a tendency to build up an "energetic resistance" when something is "pushed" against for too long. Rather than swing a hammer once and just keep pressing hard against a nail, we get better results by *alternating* our *efforts* with *repetitive* swings.

To be effective, *systematic processing* is applied to only one thing/area at a time. It is for this reason that a *Pilot* must be aware of where a *Seeker's attention* is *fixed*—or a *Solo-Pilot* must be aware of it. If it *is* "stuck" on a point that can't be put aside enough to do something else, then it must be addressed first in *processing*, because that is the *fixed* point of *attention* that all other *processing* will take place from anyways. The *"presence"* that is elsewhere must be brought under *control* before other gains will be made *"in-session."*

There are some procedures we present as *processing,* but which are really *"exercises"* that may not have a specific *"end-point"* — for example: practicing a skill or ability with *"repetitive doing."* These are often referred to as *"objective processes"* since they pertain to the *"external environment,"* even when practiced mentally — such as: *"Spot three points outside the building"* (which is alternated with *"three points in the room"*).

Most general *processes,* which get a *Seeker* to *confront* things, are *"repetitive"* in style. The goal is to push *through* something — some perceived *barrier* — or else *"uncover"* something to reveal *deeper* and *deeper* layers, until you can *"spot"* a basic *"answer"* (or *"confront"* an underlying *"incident"*), at which, the 'area' becomes *defragmented.*

A more specific type of *process* might require going through a "prepared list" of "items" (*terminals* or *areas*) to see which is the most "turbulent" or "reactive." For example: terminals for the *"Spheres of Ex-*

istence" might be listed ("*Self,*" "*Home,*" "*Family,*" "*Groups,*" &tc.) and the goal is to find the *most correct answer*. It may be that the *Seeker* is already *knowingly aware* of the "*answer.*" But a more "*systematic*" approach is to apply *Biofeedback* (*e.g. GSR-Meter*) and see what "reacts" (or gives the largest "*read*" on the *device*).

GSR-devices may also indicate sources of underlying *fragmentation* that the *Seeker* is not already aware of. But, it is important not to treat the *device* itself as some kind of "*oracle.*" It simply allows a *Pilot* to *see* "*reactive-responses*" with electronic precision—not altogether different than the instruments used for *piloting an aircraft*.

Another underlying fundamental to our *systematic processing* involves having a *Seeker* do *knowingly* what they are already doing on *automatic* (or as an *automatic response*). This helps *Seekers* practice regaining full conscious *control*. On the surface, to an outsider, some might argue that elements of *hypnotism* are present here; and they would be half right. We are actually doing the *reverse* of *hypnotism*; and the "duplication" of the "automation" is also only one part of the procedure.

When working to regain *control* of something *operating* on *automatic*, the *Seeker* is already starting from a *hypnotic-like* point of *fixation* and *unknowingness*. It is, after all, their own *creations*, *copies* and *mechanisms* that are still *persisting* and *operating automatically*.

Only when a *Seeker* is *certain* that they have full *control* of "*doing*" or "*creating*" something *knowingly* "at will," can they give up the "hold" on the *automation* and not feel a sense of "loss."

If you *suppress* what is happening on *automatic*, a *Seeker* won't "let go" of it and it may get buried deeper. Then you end up with a *persistence* of both the *suppression* and the *automation* to handle.

The second part of this procedure is for a *Seeker* to alternately increase and decrease the *automated action*, rather than putting all *attention* forcefully on "stopping." In this wise, you would repeatedly alternate exaggerating the condition "worse," and then making it "better," until you can *systematically* regain full *control*.

"*Creativeness Processing*" involves practice with *creating mental imagery*. Our underlying *spiritual ability* (and native function) is "*To Create*." Some interestingly effective *processes* simply require a *Seeker* to *knowingly* "create" things under their *control*. If you *create* something *causatively*, then you don't have to *compulsively (on automatic)*.

For example: if *obsessively* worried about something, or there is a "*stuck picture*" (or "*imprint*"), then a *Seeker knowingly/intentionally* "*creates*" (or "*Imagines*") many "*copies*" (and alterations thereof) until the *mental imagery* is fully under their *control* (and no longer *reactive/persistent*).

Not only does the *persistent condition* get lessened; the ability to *confront* "it" (or the situation), increases. Withdrawing from it has a tendency to "pull in" or "manifest" more of what we don't want. By demonstrating a *willingness* to *create it*, there is an "out-flow" of energy in that area and no perceived "deficiency" or "loss" to be filled by unwanted/undesirable *creations*.

This procedure is only effective if a *Seeker* does *not* attempt to change (or alter) the actual "reactive" (or *imprinted*) *mental image* directly. This method requires one's own *conscious creation*; not an automatically generated *imprint* or *"old picture."*

To be *certain* of this: a *Seeker* should make/*create* many "*copies*"; not just one. The *copies* may then be altered—their color, size, location, &tc. may be changed—in whatever ways are necessary for a *Seeker* to be certain that these "images" are *their own creation* and fully under *their own control.*

Full *responsibility* and *control* of *creation* also requires a *willingness* to handle the other side of it: *destruction* or "uncreation." *Fragmentation* in this area alone is enough to hinder *creative ability*.

Of course, when one *knows* they can *recreate* at *will*, there is no reason to restrict *freedom* with a *persistence*. Our "stuck" (or "fixed") *attention-units* (*Awareness*) serve us much better when "*free*" and under our own total *conscious control* once again.

Although it is usually not problematic in *processes*, "*Create*" and "*Destroy*" are both "*hot buttons*" that have a potential to trigger (or *restimulate*) *turbulent fragmentation*. At *upper-levels*, we know this is because both are *keywords* (or *buttons*) used for "*spiritual implant platforms*." Each of us is likely to have *some charge* on these words.

As a general rule for any procedure used:

> *Once a process starts to run,*
> *continue it until it is done.*

While a *process* is *run*, other things often come into view, and there is a tendency to start chasing after those things rather than completing the original *process*. If something does come up: make a note of it to handle later in a separate *process*, and continue what you're doing. Otherwise, no *processing* will actually happen; you will just be following one "thought-trail" after another, rather than *processing* them.

The *"Pathway to Ascension" Professional Course* material demonstrates to a *Seeker* how to apply all of these *systematic procedures* to specific areas of their life. Getting "started" *in-session* is covered in the *Basic Course, Lesson-6, "Systemology Processing."* The real issue that we want to discuss here is: knowing when to "stop."

End-points of a *process* (and/or *session*) are when there is a "win"—a point of "gain" or "improvement." It may not be the total *"end-realization"* of a *"level,"* or some huge "breakthrough" every time; but in order to keep making stable progress: you need to *acknowledge the wins* as they happen.

It's a mistake to "push" too hard and too long on a *process,* hoping to achieve some "major advancement" meanwhile *invalidating* the actual *wins* along the way that may have gone unnoticed. Because they weren't *acknowledged* as such, the *process* ran "past" or "over" the point that one should have stopped. Once that layer of *realization* or *defragmentation* is established (assuming things still feel incomplete), then you continue in a later *process* or *session,* working from those stable gains.

The *"eureka"* or *"this is it!"* moments are critical to *acknowledge* along the way in order to establish the stability and certainty. *Invalidating,* or blowing past, these moments will interfere with further progress. We *"chisel"* away at an area of *fragmentation* until that critical point when it simply "cracks" and falls away. There is no absolute determination about which *process* (or for "how long") it will take for this to occur. But in order for it to occur, successful *chiseling* must be *acknowledged* as *actually happening*—as *reality*.

Defragmentation is a gradual process of relieving the "weight" off of the *Spirit*. This "weight" is mostly *persistently created entangled energy-masses*. A proper "*session*" should provide *some sense of release* to a *Seeker* for it to be effective.

If a *process* is not *run long enough*, there is a general feeling of "incompleteness." A *Seeker* may feel irritable as a result. When first learning, *Solo-Pilots* often don't *run* a *process* long enough. This is why good record-keeping (or "*Flight-Logs*") are important. Because, if this is determined to be the case, the simple solution is to spot the incomplete *process* and finish it. Irritability and hopeless feelings are good indicators for a *process* being "*under-run*."

The other side of this—"*over-run*"—tends

to make things more *"solid"* or feel *"heavier."* Usually an area or target item was *defragmented* (a *release-point* was achieved) but since the *process* continues to target it as *being there*, it gets "pulled in" again, or else is *recreated.* This happens when a beginner expects a single *process* to handle everything, or do it all, when it really requires applying many different *processes*, each providing another step forward as a fairly quick progression.

Solo-Pilots are encouraged to go through the material of the *Professional Course* in a swift manner, with the expectation that the *Seeker* will make multiple passes over certain areas, rather than lingering on one *process* or *procedure* too long.

The *systematic* solution to an *"over-run" process* is to simply *"spot"* and *acknowledge* the point when the *"win"* or *"new realization"* had occurred (but was overlooked, not *acknowledged*, and *invalidated*).

PREVENTATIVE FUNDAMENTALS

If a *Seeker* has an *upset*, a *problem*, or any *attention* "stuck" on things they are worried about, it is not possible to progress in other areas until this handled. In the *Professional Course*, this handling is called "preventative fundamentals" because a *Pilot* must take care of these things first before attempting to spend *session* time in other areas. What we are *preventing* is an *invalidation* of our methods by a *Seeker* that is unable to apply *presence* of *attention in-session*. These fundamentals are treated in *Professional Course* materials:

1. A *break* or *upset* in the "*Flow-Factors*" — enforced or inhibited *communication*, *likingness* and/or *agreement*. [*Lesson-7*, "*Eliminating Barriers*"]

2. A "*Human Problem*" — present-time *attention* (*presence*) is occupied fixedly

elsewhere (and outside one's own control). [*Lesson-4, "Handling Humanity"*]

3. A *"Hold-Out"* — *attention* restimulated an area, usually because someone else *almost found out* about it. [*Lesson-6, "Escaping Spirit-Traps"*]

A *Solo-Pilot* looks over this list and determines if any of these factors are in play at the start of a *session*. In *Traditional Piloting*, a *GSR-Meter* may be used to *assess* if anything on the list *reads*. For example:

1. "Is there a *break* or *upset* of a *Flow-Factor?*"

[if it *"reads,"* check]

   a. "Is there a break in *Communication?*"

   b. "On *Likingness?*"

   c. "On *Agreement?*"

[then, *run* on what *"reads"*]

   a. "Was this ___ *Enforced?*"

   b. *"Inhibited?"*

In this first case: when you can *spot* the primary underlying source of the *upset* — such as *"inhibited communication"* or *"enforced agreement"* — there should be *some* feeling of *"relief."* If not: you may need to *reassess* the list.

The *"relief on spotting"* is either partial or total. If total: *acknowledge* it and continue on with the *session.* If partial: handle the *upset* (or *flow-break*) before continuing. It is handled by *spotting* the *flow* and *circuit.*

For example: did *you inhibit (or enforce) someone else's communication (&tc.)* or did *someone else inhibit yours?* Perhaps it was observing *someone else inhibiting another.* Whatever the case: *identify it*, then *spot* exactly what *communication* was *inhibited.* Then *spot* yourself in the situation; what you *did* and *decided* as a result of it, *&tc*. If the *turbulence* doesn't resolve or worsens: look for an earlier incident that was similar. If it gets more *solid,* it has been *overrun*: *spot* the *release-point* that was missed.

PSYCHOSOMATICS & PAIN

Generally speaking: applying *systemology* to treat *"pain"* is an *advanced* practice. It is important to know that there will be a moment when the *pain* becomes sharper before it *releases*. This is because you have to remove a *mental barrier* that *suppresses* the *pain* in order to *confront it "As-It-Is."*

Such practices are not applied to *injury emergencies* — when other *"first aid"* is required for the *Body*; but they can greatly assist thereafter. Long-term use of *pain-suppression drugs* can interfere with abilities to handle *pain* with mental techniques.

The basic *"touch-back"* technique is given in the first *Professional Course (PC)* lesson. [See also *PC Lesson-5, 9* and *10*.] Although physical injury includes "loss" or "damage" to *cells*, the *pain*-sensation generated by the *"reactive control-center"* of the *Mind* is generally perceived as more extreme than what it actually is or should be.

Some *90%* (or more) of what you feel as *"pain"* is really due to a *mental accumulation* of *"past pains,"* rather than that actual present-time moment. It accumulates like *imprint-chains*; in this case, *mental images* or *impressions* of the *pain.* It was once believed that all this information was only *imprinted* as *"engram memories"* onto a living *cell*. At *upper-levels*, we realize this is only one part of the whole situation.

The subject of *"Spiritual Machinery"* is introduced in *PC Lesson-14.* We have parts of our *Awareness* hidden away, *compulsively creating machinery*, much of which is intimately connected to the *Body*. This is why when the *Body* "stubs" *its toe*, you get a sense that *you* "stubbed" *your toe.* The *machinery* detects the physical action and generates the *pain*-sensation for you to experience as *reality.*

An individual can also get *restimulated* by the environment (or a particular thought) and trigger this *machinery* to generate a *pain*-sensation. Even if no physical impact occurred to cause it, the same *impression* is sensed as *real*; the same *machinery* has been activated as if an injury is present. Any *systematic procedure* for this would require getting more of that *machinery* under the *Seeker's conscious control*.

The *advanced technique* (*exercise*) for handling *pain, sensation, emotion*, or even *drug effects*, is to practice placing (*whatever it is*) into walls, floors, ceilings, or large objects in view. In this wise, we do not "stop" or "suppress" the *machinery*; we do not try to leave ourselves numb. We *redirect* the *flow* (with *intention/attention*) to locations *external* to the *Body*. We *confront it As-It-Is*, but while it's being directed "*over there.*"

Much like other collected "experiences" or *creations* discussed in this manual: an individual won't be able to fully let go of something unless they are certain it can be *recreated* at *will*. This includes *sensations*; even undesirable ones. *Machinery* is a form of *automation*; so "procedures" for regaining *control* of it can apply here too.

Our *advanced technique* is not particularly *easy*—particularly if being practiced for the first time during an extreme situation. The exercise should be practiced on *emotions* first; gaining more *control* over *emotional machinery*, while also earning more experience with these procedures.

When first practicing, a *Seeker* may only get the vaguest sense or an *imagined* idea that there is a faint *sensation* in the "*wall*." Just keep practicing with this. Also, don't concentrate too hard on just one particular point on the "*wall*." This works best when briskly moving from spot to spot, alternating between spots, or simply going around the room. Use all six basic directions; not just the "*wall*" in front of you.

After a *Seeker* is successful employing this "*wall*"-technique with significant results, if additional handling is required, gradient steps for improving *machinery control* (directing it into the "*walls*" &tc.) are:

A. Alternate: *spots near* to and *far* from the *Body* (including *large objects*).

B. Alternate: *spots* in the *walls* and *spots* inside the *Body* (but not where the *pain* actually is).

C. Alternate: *spots* in the *walls* and *spots* inside the *Body* (where it actually is).

D. Alternate: *spots* where it is and *spots* where it isn't (inside the *Body*).

With the total sensation being moved *on* and *off* the *spot* in the *Body*, greater *control* should occur. This does not treat all of the underlying issues of, for example, what *imprints* and *postulates* may be activating various *machinery*. That still requires other *processing*; but if a *Seeker's attention* is mostly fixed on *pain*, then that condition must be handled first as a fundamental.

There is another *advanced technique* (that requires *Systemology Level-6* proficiency). It involves making many *facsimile-copies* of a sensation (preferably out to *infinity* as practiced with the *Professional Course*) on opposite sides of an injured or painful area; then pushing them into the *Body* simultaneously; doing this many times from multiple axis/directions.

A *Seeker* makes certain to *alter* their *copies* to make sure they are *their creation.* Start with one pair of *copies* until you can make them in "batches" (and preferably out to *infinity*).

The trick is to stay determined. This isn't applied at *lower-levels* because of the *ability-to-confront* (*Awareness*) that is required. The chronic sensations come off in layers, *resurfacing* each similar occurrence for this particular *Body* until the first injury or *pain*-incident is contacted.

The *perception* of *sensation* can shift fairly

quickly; but you continue until it feels like you've hit the basic one. When that one falls away and you feel better, you *end* the *process*. *Running* it even one PCL longer may pull in sensations for that area from an earlier *Body* you once used.

This technique can also be practiced with making *copies* of entire areas of the *Body*, not just the sensation itself. Another trick to it is that when one layer of sensation (or incident) falls away, you *acknowledge* it and switch *attention* to the same area on the other side of the *Body*, repeating the same with *copies* of whatever is there. If there is no sensation felt there, just *copy* the physical structure (area) that *is* there. Then you can switch back to the original side you were treating (if layers remain).

SPIRITUAL IMPLANTS & ENTITIES

In *PC Lesson-11*, we introduce *"Spiritual Implants."* Handling these *heavy conditioning incidents* (and their *effects*) is a significant part of *Systemology Level-7* and above. The subject of *Entities* is treated at *Level-8*.

In *this Physical Universe*, *Implants* are laid in by *force* and *electronic waves*. In earlier *Universes*, before *Alpha-Spirits* considered they could be hurt, *Implanting* included using *aesthetic waves*, *emotion* and *symbols* to embed/encode *false information*.

Implants consist of a *systematic sequence* of *considerations* or *postulates* (*Alpha Thought*) that are intentionally *"charged/fragmented"* in order to *control* an individual's *reality*. We *process-out* these thought-intentions as *"command-items."* They are not our original thoughts, but they are reinforced with a *charge* as if they *are* our own intentions.

Implants often contain a repeating *pattern* of opposing *"items."* Some *Implants* are more complex, using repeating *patterns* within other *patterns* on a declining scale. We refer to a single *sequence* of the complete *pattern* as an *"Implant Platform."* It provides a *"plane," "surface"* or *"filter"* for an area, which affects later *fragmentation.*

An *Implant Platform* may contain over *100* *"command-items"* —each of which requires *defragmentation* in *sequence.* For this reason, standard procedures at *advanced levels* utilize a *Biofeedback Device.* A *Platform* list is *processed-out* by repeatedly *"spotting"* a *"command-item"* until it ceases to *read* on a *GSR-Meter*; then, going to the next *item* and doing the same.

Some basic techniques for *defragmenting Implants"* are given in *PC Lesson-11.* For *Level-5*, without a *GSR-Meter*, the most basic procedure is:

A. *"Spot (or Imagine) an implant-item (or command-item in the listed sequence)."*

B. *"Confront it until it ceases to have any effect."*

The easiest way for a *Seeker* to accomplish this is to alternately:

A. *"Spot the implanted command-item."*

B. *"Spot something in the room."*

"Command-Items" are/were not *implanted* in "English" (or any language of Human speech). Therefore, the best we can do for *processing* is to *"approximate"* their meaning (*get a sense* for their original *intention*) when each *"command-item"* is *"Spotted."*

When a *GSR-Meter* is applied to this practice, then *"Step-B"* is technically replaced with *"Spotting the Meter display for reads."*

A *Seeker* *"Spots"* the *"item"* and then immediately checks the *Meter* for a *"read."* It is best if the *list* and the *Meter* are next to each other, in easy view. This continues, alternating *attention* between the "item" and the *Meter* until no "*charge*" is *reading.*

Simply reading through an *item-list* is not sufficient to *process-out* the *significances.* Just staring at an *item* doesn't do much good either. *Attention* shifts "*on*" and "*off*" an *item* is what is required. Some reasons for this are explained previously in this manual. In some cases it may be beneficial to *alternate* between *two* directly "opposing" *items*; also called a "*pair.*" And when that *pair* is *defragmented*, you go to the next *pair*. But not all *Implant-Platforms* are designed with *item-pairs.*

Implant-handling is always *Piloted Solo.* If a *Seeker* runs into excessive *turbulence* doing so, a *systematic* solution is to *spot* the beginning of the *Implant* or *incident*. That means the first *item* on the list; or even the events of the *incident* leading up to the *Implant*. It is for this reason that the "*Entry-Into-This-Universe*" (or *Heaven Im-*

plant) is the first one that a *Seeker* is introduced to (*PC Lesson-11*). Being the first one used for *this Physical Universe*, it may be *spotted* to relieve some *pressure* off of more recent *Implant-Platforms* or *incidents*.

This specific *entry-incident* applies only to *this Physical Universe*. Each *Universe* has its own *Entry-Point Implant* to assign the *reality-parameters* of *that Universe*. Each *incident* makes an *impression* that *it* is the "*Beginning of Time*," but it is really only the beginning of an *Alpha-Spirit's* experience within *that Universe*. Note that *spotting* such things does not *defragment* more recent *Implants*, but it is powerful enough to pull *attention* away from *restimulation* that working with *Implants* might trigger.

As a *false* "*Beginning of Time*," each *entry-incident* also *Implants* a *false* "native state" for an *Alpha-Spirit*—meaning a *Beingness* or "*purpose*" impressed as an individual's own original and basic function. For example: in *this Physical Universe*, the basic game-goal is: *"To Survive."* This is laid in with an *Implanting-Incident* that also reinforces an idea that we must compete with each other to retain this "native state." Everything about the *Implant* is a "lie," but it sets up the *game* we experience in this version of *Beta-Existence.*

The earliest known *Implant-Series* appears to set up the structure for everything else. It is referred to as the *"Jewel of Knowledge"* and is treated at *Systemology Level-7.* An understanding of all these *Implants* is critical for handling *Entities* at *Level-8.* The purpose of an *Implant* is to get an *Alpha-Spirit* to *compulsively create* a *condition,* including the *Universe* they're experiencing.

The subjects of *Entities* is not introduced early on the *Pathway* for the same reason as *Spiritual Implants.* These areas require a *high-level Awareness* and *ability-to-confront.* It is also important for a *Seeker* to regain a certain degree of *Self-determination* and the ability to properly *identify "conditions"* and "*sources.*" Otherwise we will improperly assign all "*cause*" to *external* factors, and lose *responsibility* and *control* of handling our *fragmented creations.*

Entities have very little ability to affect us directly. They are *subtle facets* of our more *visible* environment with an equal ability to "trigger," *restimulate*, or otherwise remind us of unpleasant things. More details on handling *Entities* is given in the *Advanced Training Course* material for *Systemology Level-8.*

SOLO-PILOTING UPPER-LEVELS

Professional Pilots are trained at the *Mardukite Academy of Systemology* using the *Systemology Core Research Volumes.* While our new *Professional Course* sidesteps the requirement of a *Co-Pilot*, it does not replace all of the knowledge that goes with that role.

Our *Basic, Professional,* and *Advanced* materials are all expertly designed for the greatest effectiveness and conciseness. It does not, however, provide *all* of the information that is available on the various subjects. Since every student may not have time available to study all the background research, these *Advanced Supplements* have been prepared. However, if a *Solo-Pilot* still finds a certain area difficult to understand, they should refer to the *Systemology Core Research Volumes.*

Although *Solo-Piloting* does not carry the same two-person element as *Traditional Piloting*, the same rules apply to the *Processing Communication Cycle* (see *"Metahuman Destinations: Volume One"*), and are particularly critical when treating *upper levels* and *Flying-Solo* with a *GSR-Meter.*

Upper-level materials will provide instructions, *"processing command-lines"* (*"PCL"*), and/or *"command-items"* (for *Implants*). A *Solo-Pilot* must understand the *command*

and *procedures* before *running* anything as a *process.*

The *Seeker* then concentrates and silently *intends* the PCL as a *communication* from *Self*-to-*Self.* If there is "*charge*" on it, then there is an *answer* or *response (reaction)*. By paying *attention* to this *answer,* there is an *acknowledgment*—and that *ends* one complete *communication cycle.*

Biofeedback Devices can play a role in *Solo-Piloting* to assist recognizing when *charge* on an *item* is present—even if "beneath the surface" and not otherwise noticed. When there is no longer a *meter-read,* that is *acknowledged* as an *end-cycle* for the PCL.

Unlike *Traditional Piloting,* a *Solo-Pilot* will rarely employ spoken PCL. In fact, starting with *Systemology Level-5,* more of the *processing* operates purely on an *intention* or *Alpha-Thought* level. If using a *GSR-Meter,* a *Seeker* must be able to both read a PCL and keep an eye on a *meter* for *reads.*

It is important to catch the *first read* on an *item*, because some *items* may not give a second *read* immediately afterward. This is another reason we prefer to shift *attention* "*on*" and "*off*" an *item*. But unless a *Seeker* catches the *first read*, it may *invalidate* the remaining *process*. It is also helpful to practice the skill of "*seeing*" something as if for the *first time*.

If your model of *GSR-Meter* requires using *two electrodes* (*one* for each hand), then it has to be modified for *Solo-Piloting*. All that needs to be done is make it so both *electrodes* can be held in one hand, in order to properly operate the *Meter* knobs. In most cases, the two *electrodes* are like hollow metal "*cans*" that can be attached with a *spacer* or empty *paper-towel roll* (to keep the two *electrodes* from touching, or else *short-circuiting*).

There is another *advanced* matter in these areas that must also be addressed. When a *Seeker* has reached *upper-level processing*, their *Awareness* has improved; their ability to affect the *Mind* with *intention* and *Alpha-Thought* is much stronger. This also means they've developed an ability to *intentionally* affect *Meter-reads*.

During a *Solo-session*: if a PCL *reads*, but a *Seeker* knows they had instantly thought "NO!" as a response, you can easily just check (with the *Meter*) "*Did the PCL read on 'No'?*" It might *read* again, which will confirm this, so you *acknowledge* "It read on 'No'," and continue your *processing*.

* * * * * * *

The information in this procedural manual should assist a *Seeker* and *Pilot* in better understanding the *systematic* methods we use for all *processing-levels* of the *Pathway*. Studying this material thoroughly allows both the *Professional Course* and *Advanced Training Course* to be more effectively applied. Use the manuals and lessons as intended and you will do just fine. *See you on the other side!*

APPENDIX: THE FORMAL SESSION

1. <u>BEGINNING THE SESSION</u>

"Would it be okay with you if we begin this session now?"

"Okay."

"Start of session."

2. <u>OPENING PROCEDURES</u>

A. Presence In-Session

"Is there anything going on that might keep your attention from being present in-session?"

(if *"no,"* acknowledge and go to *B.*; if *"yes,"* continue below)

"Okay. Tell me about it."

"Alright. How does that problem seem to you now?"

(if *"further away"* or handled, acknowledge and go to *B.*; if *"closer"* or more turbulent, continue below)

"Spot something in the incident; Spot something in the room."

(this alternating command line is repeated as needed)

B. Orientation in Present Space-Time

"Get the sense of you making that body sit in that chair."

"Okay. Get a sense of the floor beneath your feet."

"Do you have that real good?"

(if *"no,"* acknowledge and repeat *A.*; if *"yes,"* continue below)

"Recall a time something seemed real to you."

"Tell me something you notice about it."

"Look around and spot something in the room."

"What do you notice about that?"

(these last four command lines are repeated in series as needed; acknowledge and continue below)

C. Control of Body and Mind In-Session

(two dissimilar objects—here given as "*Item-1*" and "*Item-2*"—are presented and placed within reach; or alternatively, at two distant points in the room, in which a command line for "walking" between them would be inserted)

"*Pick up Item-1.*"

"*Tell me about its weight.*"

"*Tell me about its color.*"

"*Tell me about its texture.*"

"*Put it down.*"

"*Pick up Item-2.*"

"*Tell me about its weight.*"

"*Tell me about its color.*"

"*Tell me about its texture.*"

"*Put it down.*"

(this series of command-lines may be repeated several times; when there is no communication-lag for several full series, and duplicate answers are reoccurring, acknowledge and continue below)

"Choose an object. Decide when you are going to reach for it. Then make that body pick it up."

"Now decide when you are going to put it down. Then make that body put it back where it was."

(repeat as needed; when there is no communication-lag for a full series of command lines, acknowledge and continue below)

"Close your eyes. Put all of your attention on the upper two back corners of the room and just get real interested in them for a while."

(if there are no visible signs of "strain" after two minutes, acknowledge and continue below)

D. Establishing the Session

"Do you have any goals for this session, or anything in particular you want to address?"

(acknowledge, then start a process)

3. STARTING A PROCESS

"I would like to start a process; would that be okay?"

"Alright. The command lines are ---. Does this make sense?"

(if *"no,"* clear up any misunderstood words; if *"yes,"* start the process)

4. <u>CHANGING A PROCESS</u>

(only the wording in a command line may be changed to make it more workable for a *Seeker*; to change processes altogether, the present process must reach an end-point)

Example: a Seeker expresses inability to "imagine" or visualize imagery.

"Okay. Well, just 'get a sense' of..." or *"Just 'get the idea' of..."*

Example: a Seeker expresses discomfort (or withdrawal from) recalling a particular incident.

"That's fine. What part of that incident 'could' you confront?"

5. <u>STOPPING A PROCESS</u>

(when an end-point has been reached on a repetitive-style process)

"We'll just run this process a couple more times if that's okay with you?"

(general process is run two more times)

"Okay. Is there anything you would like to tell me before we end this process?"

(**or**, if an end-point "realization" is communicated from a process)

"Alright. Very good."

(the formal end of a particular process requires a command-line)

"End of process."

6. ENDING THE SESSION

(once a process, or series of processes, is completed)

"Is there anything you would like to tell me before we end this session?"

(if "yes," acknowledge and handle it with communication before ending the session; if "no," continue below)

"Would it be okay if we ended this session now?"

"Okay."
"End of session."

GLOSSARY

actualization : to make actual, not just potential; to bring into full solid Reality; to realize fully in *Awareness* as a "thing."

agreement (reality) : unanimity of opinion of what is "thought" to be known; an accepted arrangement of how things are; things we consider as "real" or as an "is" of "reality"; a consensus of what is real as made by standard-issue (common) participants; what an individual contributes to or accepts as "real"; in *Systemology*, a synonym for "*reality.*"

alpha : the first, primary, basic, superior or beginning of some form; in *Systemology*, referring to the state of existence operating on spiritual archetypes and postulates, will and intention "exterior" to the low-level condensation and solidarity of energy and matter as the 'physical universe' (*beta*).

alpha-spirit : a "spiritual" *Life*-form; the "true" *Self* or I-AM; the *individual*; the spiritual (*alpha*) *Self* that is animating the (*beta*) physical body or "*genetic vehicle*" using a continuous *Lifeline* of spiritual ("*ZU*") energy; an individual spiritual (*alpha*) entity possessing no physical mass or measurable waveform (motion) in the *Physical Universe* as itself, so it animates the (*beta*) physical body or "*genetic vehicle*" as a catalyst to experience *Self*-determined causality in effect within the *Physical Universe*; a singular unit or point of *Spiritual Awareness* that is *Aware* that it is *Aware*.

alpha thought : the highest spiritual *Self-determination* over creation and existence exercised by an Alpha-Spirit; the Alpha range of pure *Creative Ability* based on direct postulates and considerations of *Beingness*; spiritual qualities comparable to "thought" but originating in Alpha-existence, independently superior to a Mind-System.

ascension : actualized *Awareness* elevated to the point of true "spiritual existence" exterior to *beta existence*. An "Ascended Master" is one who has returned to an incarnation on Earth as an inherently *Enlightened One*, demonstrable in their words and actions; they have the ability to *Self-direct* the "Mind" and "Body" as *Self* (as a "Spirit"); and to maintain consciousness as a personal identity continuum with the same *Self-directed* control and communication of Will-Intention that is exercised, actualized and developed deliberately during one's present incarnation.

associative knowledge : significance or meaning of a facet or aspect assigned to (or considered to have) a direct relationship with another facet; to connect or relate ideas or facets of existence with one another; in traditional systems logic, an equivalency of significance or meaning between facets or sets that are grouped together, such as in $(a + b) + c = a + (b + c)$; in Systemology, erroneous associative knowledge is assignment of the same value to all facets or parts considered as related (even when they are not actually so), such as in $a = a$, $b = a$, $c = a$ and so forth without distinction.

attention : active use of *Awareness* toward a specific aspect or thing; the act of "attending" with the presence of *Self*; a direction of focus or concentration of *Awareness* along a particular channel or conduit or toward a particular terminal node or communication termination point; the Self-directed concentration of personal energy as a combination of observation, thought-waves and consideration; focused application of *Self-Directed Awareness*.

awareness : the highest sense of-and-as *Self* in knowing and being as I-AM (the *Alpha-Spirit*); the extent of beingness directed as a viewpoint (POV) experienced by *Self* as *Knowingness*.

beta (awareness) : all consciousness activity ("*Awareness*") in the "Physical Universe" (KI, in *Zuism*) or else in *beta-existence*; *Awareness* within the range of the *genetic-body*, including material thoughts, emotional responses and physical motors; personal *Awareness* of physical energy and physical matter moving through physical space and experienced as "time"; the *Awareness* held by *Self* that is restricted to an organic *Lifeform* or "*genetic vehicle*" in which it experiences causality in *beta-existence*.

beta (existence) : all manifestation in the "Physical Universe" (KI, in *Zuism*); the conditions of *Awareness* for the *Alpha-spirit* (*Self*) as a physical organic *Lifeform* or "*genetic vehicle*" in which it experiences causality in the *Physical Universe*.

charge : to fill or furnish with a quality; to supply with energy; to lay a command upon; in *Systemology*—to imbue with intention; to overspread with emotion; personal energy stores and significances entwined as fragmentation in mental images, reactive-response encoding and intellectual (and/or) programmed beliefs.

channel : a specific stream, course, current, direction or route; to form or cut a groove or ridge or otherwise guide along a specific course; a direct path; an artificial aqueduct created to connect two water bodies or water or make travel possible.

circuit : a circular path or loop; a closed-path within a system that allows a flow; a pattern or action or wave movement that follows a specific route or potential path only; in *Systemology*, "*communication processing*" pertaining to a specific *flow* of energy or information along a channel; "*feedback loop.*"

communication : successful transmission of information, data, energy (&tc.) along a message line, with a reception of feedback; an energetic flow of intention to cause an effect (or duplication) at a distance; the personal energy moved or acted upon by will or else 'selective directed attention'; the 'messenger action' used to transmit and receive energy across a medium; also relay of energy, a message or signal—or even locating a personal POV (viewpoint) for the Self—along the *ZU-line*.

condense (condensation) : the transition of vapor to liquid; denoting a change in state to a more substantial or solid condition; leading to a more compact or solid form.

confront : to come around in front of; to be in the presence of; to stand in front of, or in the face of; to meet "face-to-face" or "face-up-to"; additionally, in *Systemology*, to fully tolerate or acceptably withstand an encounter with a particular manifestation without an automatic reactive response.

consideration : careful analytical reflection of all aspects; deliberation; determining the significance of a "thing" in relation to similarity or dissimilarity to other "things"; evaluation of facts and importance of certain facts; thorough examination of all aspects related to, or important for, making a decision; the analysis of consequences and estimation of significance when making decisions; also in *Systemology*, the *postulate* or *Alpha-Thought* that defines the state of *beingness* for what something "*is.*"

defragmentation : the *reparation* of wholeness; collecting all dispersed parts to reform an original whole; a process of removing "*fragmentation*" in data or knowledge to provide a clear understanding; applying techniques and processes that promote a *holistic* interconnected *alpha* state, favoring observational *Awareness* of continuity in all spiritual and physical systems; in *Systemology*, a "*Seeker*" achieving actualized "*Self-Honest Awareness*" is said to be in a basic state of *beta-defragmentation*, whereas *Alpha-defragmentation* is the rehabilitation of the *creative ability*, managing the *Spiritual Timeline* and the POV of *Self* as Alpha-Spirit (I-AM).

existence : the *state* or fact of *apparent manifestation*; the resulting combination of the Principles of Manifestation: consciousness, motion and substance; continued *survival*; that which independently exists.

exterior : outside of; on the outside; in *Systemology*, we mean specifically the POV of *Self* that is *'outside of'* the *Human Condition,* free of the physical and mental trappings of the Physical Universe; a metahuman range of consideration; see also *'Zu-Vision'*.

external : a force coming from outside; information received from outside sources; in *Systemology*, the objective *'Physical Universe'* existence, or *beta-existence*, that the Physical Body or *genetic vehicle* is essentially *anchored* to for its considerations of locational space-time as a dimension or POV.

fragmentation : breaking into parts and scattering the pieces; the *fractioning* of wholeness or the *fracture* of a holistic interconnected *alpha* state, favoring observational *Awareness* of perceived connectivity between parts; *discontinuity*; separation of a totality into parts; in *Systemology*, a person outside of *Self-Honesty* is said to be operating from a *fragmented* state.

flow : movement across (or through) a channel (or conduit); a direction of active energetic motion, typically distinguished as either an *in-flow*, *out-flow* or *cross-flow*.

genetic-vehicle : a physical *Life*-form; the physical (*beta*) body that is animated/controlled by the (*Alpha*) *Spirit* using a continuous *Spiritual Lifeline* (ZU); a physical (*beta*) organic receptacle and catalyst for the (*Alpha*) *Self* to operate "causes" and experience "effects" within the *Physical Universe*.

harmful-act : a counter-survival mode of behavior or action (esp. that causes harm to one of more *Spheres of Existence*)—or—an overtly aggressive (hostile and/or destructive) action against an individual or any other *Sphere of Existence*; in *Utilitarian Systemology*—a short-sighted (serves fewest/lowest *Spheres of Existence*) intentional overtly harmful action to resolve a perceived problem; a revision of the rule for standard *Utilitarianism* for Systemology to distinguish actions which provide the least benefit to the least number of *Spheres of Existence*, or else the greatest harm to the greatest number of *Spheres of Existence*; in *moral philosophy*—an action which can be experienced by few and/or which one would not be willing to experience for themselves (*theft, slander, rape, &tc*); an iniquity or iniquitous act.

hold-back : withheld communications (esp. actions) such as "*Hold-Outs*"; intentional (or automatic) withdrawal (as opposed to reach); Self-restraint (which may eventually be enforced or automated); not reaching, acting or expressing, when one should be; an ability that is now restrained (on automatic) due to inability to withhold it on Self-determinism alone.

hold-outs : in photography, the numerous snapshots/pictures withheld from the final display or professional presentation of the event; withheld communications; in Utilitarian Systemology— energetic withdrawal and communication breaks with a "*terminal*" and its *Sphere of Existence* as a result of a "*Harmful-Act*"; unspoken or undiscovered (hidden, covert) actions that an individual withholds communications of, fearing punishment or endangerment of *Self-preservation* (*First Sphere*); the act of hiding (or keeping hidden) the truth of a "*Harmful-Act*"; a refusal to communicate with a *Pilot*; also "*Hold-Back*."

holistic : the examination of interconnected systems as encompassing something greater than the *sum* of their "parts."

Human Condition : a standard default state of Human experience that is generally accepted to be the extent of its potential identity (*beingness*) —currently treated as *Homo Sapiens Sapiens,* but which is scheduled for replacement by *Homo Novus* (the "New Human").

imagination : ability to create *mental imagery* in one's Personal Universe at will and change or alter it as desired; the ability to create, change and dissolve mental images on command or as an act of will; to create a mental image or have associated imagery displayed (or "conjured") in the mind that may or may not be treated as real (or memory recall) and may or may not accurately duplicate objective reality; to employ *creative abilities* of the Spirit that are independent of reality agreements with beta-existence.

imprint : to strongly impress, stamp, mark (or outline) onto a softer 'impressible' substance; to mark with pressure onto a surface; in *Systemology*, used to indicate permanent Reality impressions marked by frequencies, energies or interactions experienced during periods of emotional distress, pain, unconsciousness, loss, enforcement, or something antagonistic to physical (personal) survival, all of which are are stored with other reactive response-mechanisms at lower-levels of *Awareness* as opposed to the active memory database and proactive processing center of the Mind; an experiential "memory-set" that may later resurface—be triggered or stimulated artificially—as Reality, of which similar responses will be engaged automatically; holographic-like imagery "stamped" onto consciousness as composed of energetic *facets* tied to the "snap-shot" of an experience.

imprinting incident : the first or original event

instance communicated and *emotionally en-coded* onto an individual's "*Spiritual Timeline*" (recorded memory from all lifetimes), which formed a permanent impression that is later used to mechanistically treat future contact on that channel; the first or original occurrence of some particular *facet* or mental image related to a certain type of *encoded response*, such as pain and discomfort, losses and victimization, and even the acts that we have taken against others along the *Spiritual Timeline* of our existence that caused them to also be *Imprinted*.

intention : directed application of Will; to in-tend (have "in Mind") or signify (give "signific-ance" to) for or toward a particular purpose; in *Systemology* (from the *Standard Model*)—the spiritual activity at WILL (5.0) directed by an *Alpha Spirit* (7.0); the application of WILL as "Cause" from a higher order of Alpha Thought and consideration (6.0).

interior : inside of; on the inside; in *Systemo-logy*, we mean specifically the POV of *Self* that is fixed to the *'internal' Human Condition,* in-cluding the *Reactive Control Center* (RCC) and Mind-System or *Master Control Center* (MCC); within *beta-existence*.

internal : a force coming from inside; informa-tion received from inside sources; in *Systemo-logy*, the objective experience of *beta-existence* associated with the Physical Body or *genetic vehicle* and its POV regarding sensation and perception; from inside the body; in the body.

invalidate : decrease the level or degree or *agreement* as Reality.

mental image : a subjectively experienced "picture" created and imagined into being by the Alpha-Spirit (or at lower levels, one of its automated mechanisms) that includes all perceptible *facets* of totally immersive scene, which may be forms originated by an individual, or a "facsimile-copy" ("snap-shot") of something seen or encountered; a duplication of wave-forms in one's Personal Universe as a "picture" that mirror an "external" Universe experience, such as an *Imprint*.

perception : internalized processing of data received by the *senses*; to become *Aware of* via the senses.

pilot : a professional steersman responsible for healthy functional operation of a ship toward a specific destination; in *Systemology*, an intensive trained individual qualified to specially apply *Systemology Processing* to assist other *Seekers* on the *Pathway*.

point-of-view (POV) : a point to view from; an opinion or attitude as expressed from a specific identity-phase; a specific standpoint or vantage-point; a definitive manner of consideration specific to an individual phase or identity; a place or position affording a specific view or vantage; circumstances and programming of an individual that is conducive to a particular response, consideration or belief-set (paradigm); a position (consideration) or place (location) that provides a specific view or perspective (subjective) on experience (of the objective).

postulate : to put forward as truth; to suggest or assume an existence *to be*; to state or affirm the existence of particular conditions; to provide a basis of reasoning and belief; a basic theory accepted as fact; in *Systemology*, Alpha-Thought —the top-most decisions or considerations made by the Alpha-Spirit regarding the "*is-ness*" (what things "are") about energy-matter and space-time.

presence : a quality of some thing (*energy/matter*) being "present" in space-time; personal orientation of *Self* as an *Awareness* (*POV*) located in present space-time (environment) and communicating with extant energy-matter.

processing command line (PCL) : a directed input; a specific command using highly selective language for *Systemology Processing*; a predetermined directive statement (cause) intended to focus concentrated attention (effect).

processing, systematic : the inner-workings or "through-put" result of systems; in *Systemology*, a method of applied spiritual technology used toward personal Self-Actualization; methods of selective directed attention, communicated language and associative imagery that increases personal control of the human condition.

realization : the clear perception of an understanding; a consideration or understanding on what is "actual"; to make "real" or give "reality" to so as to grant a property of "being-ness" or "being as it is"; the state or instance of coming to an *Awareness*; in *Systemology*, "gnosis" or true knowledge achieved during *systematic processing*; achievement of a new (or higher) cognition, true knowledge or perception of Self; a consideration of reality or assignment of meaning.

responsibility : the *ability* to *respond*; the extent of mobilizing *power* and *understanding* an individual maintains as *Awareness* to enact *change*; the proactive ability to *Self-direct* and make decisions independent of an outside authority.

Seeker : an individual on the *Pathway to Self-Honesty*; a practitioner of *Mardukite Systemology* or *Systemology Processing*, that is working toward *Spiritual Ascension*.

Self-actualization : bringing the full potential of the Human spirit into Reality; expressing full capabilities and creativeness of the *Alpha-Spirit*.

Self-determinism : the freedom to act, clear of external control or influence; the personal control of Will to direct intention.

Self-honesty : the basic or original *alpha* state of *being* and *knowing*; clear and present total *Awareness* of-and-as *Self*, in its most basic and true proactive expression of itself as *Spirit* or *I-AM*—free of artificial attachments, perceptive filters and other emotionally-reactive or mentally-conditioned programming imposed on the human condition by the systematized physical world; the ability to experience existence without judgment.

spiritual timeline : a continuous stream of moment-to-moment *Mental Images* (or a record of experiences) that defines the "past" of a spiritual being (or *Alpha-Spirit*) and which includes impressions (*imprints, &tc.*) from all life-incarnations and significant spiritual events the being has encountered; in Systemology, also "*backtrack.*"

Spheres of Existence : a series of *eight* concentric circles, rings or spheres (each larger than the former) that is overlaid onto the Standard Model of Beta-Existence to demonstrate the dynamic systems of existence extending out from the POV of Self (often as a "body") at the *First Sphere*; these are given in the basic eightfold systems as: *Self*, *Home/Family*, *Groups*, *Humanity*, *Life on Earth*, *Physical Universe*, *Spiritual Universe* and *Infinity-Divinity.*

Systemology : a modern tradition of applied religious philosophy and spiritual technology based on *Arcane Tablets* (in combination with "*general systemology*" and "*games theory*") developed in the New Age underground by Joshua Free in 2011 as an advanced futurist extension of the *Mardukite Research Org.*

terminal (node) : a point, end, or mass, on a line; a connection point for closing an electric circuit, such as a post on a battery terminating at each end of its own systematic function; a point of connectivity with other points; in systems, a contact point of interaction; a point of interaction with other points.

turbulence : a quality or state of distortion or disturbance that creates irregularity of a flow or pattern; the quality or state of aberration on a line (such as ragged edges) or the emotional "turbulent feelings" attached to a particular flow or terminal node; a violent, haphazard or disharmonious commotion (such as in the ebb of gusts and lulls of wind action).

validation : a reinforcement of agreements or considerations as being "real."

viewpoint : see *"point-of-view" (POV)*.

willingness : the state of conscious Self-determined ability and interest (directed attention) to *Be*, *Do* or *Have*; a Self-determined consideration to reach, face up to (*confront*) or manage some "mass" or energy; the extent to which an individual considers themselves able to participate, act or communicate along some line, to put attention or intention on the line, or to produce (create) an effect.

ZU : the ancient Sumerian cuneiform sign for the archaic verb—*"to know,"* *"knowingness"* or *"awareness"*; in *Mardukite Zuism and Systemology*, the active energy/matter of the "Spiritual Universe" (AN) experienced as a *Lifeforce* or *consciousness* that imbues living forms extant in the "Physical Universe" (KI); *"Spiritual Life Energy"*; energy demonstrated by the WILL of an actualized *Alpha-Spirit* in the "Spiritual Universe" (AN), which impinges its *Awareness* into the Physical Universe (KI), animating/controlling *Life* for its experience of *beta-existence* along an individual Alpha-Spirit's personal *Identity-continuum*, called a *ZU-line*.

***Zu*-Line** : a theoretical construct in *Mardukite Zuism and Systemology* demonstrating *Spiritual*

Life Energy (*ZU*) as a personal individual "continuum" of Awareness interacting with all Spheres of Existence on the Standard Model of Systemology; a spectrum of potential variations and interactions of a monistic continuum or singular *Spiritual Life Energy* demonstrated on the Standard Model; an energetic channel of potential POV and "locations" of Beingness, demonstrated in early Systemology materials as an individual Alpha-Spirit's personal *Identity- continuum*, potentially connecting *Awareness* of *Self* with "*Infinity*" simultaneous with all points considered in existence; a symbolic demonstration of the "*Life-line*" on which *Awareness (ZU)* extends from the direction of the "Spiritual Universe" (AN) in its true original *alpha state* through an entire possible range of activity resulting in its *beta state* and control of a *genetic-entity* occupying the *Physical Universe (KI)*.

Zu-**Vision** : the true and basic (*Alpha*) Point-of-View (perspective, POV) maintained by *Self* as *Alpha-Spirit* outside boundaries or considerations of the *Human Condition* and *exterior* to beta-existence reality agreements with the Physical Universe; a POV of Self *as* "a unit of Spiritual Awareness" that exists independent of a "body" and entrapment in a *Human Condition*; "spirit vision" in its truest sense.

Collector's Edition Hardcover

THE FUNDAMENTALS OF
SYSTEMOLOGY

A Basic Course by
Joshua Free

*collecting material of six lesson-booklets
together in one volume!*

"Being More Than Human"

"Realities in Agreement"

"Windows To Experience"

"Ancient Systemology"

"A History of Systemology"

"Systemology Processing"

All *six* lesson-booklets of the first official
Basic Course on Mardukite Systemology
are combined together in *one volume* as
"Fundamentals of Systemology."

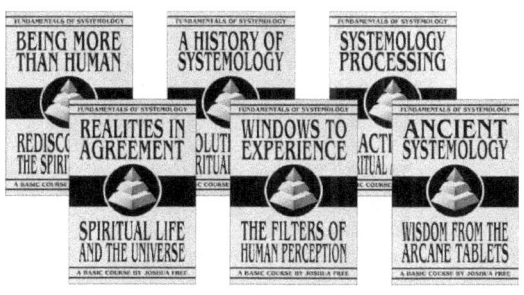

Lesson booklets are also available individually!

Collector's Edition Hardcover

THE PATHWAY TO
ASCENSION

The Official 2024 Systemology
Professional Course by
Joshua Free

All sixteen lessons available in two volumes!

"Increasing Awareness"

"Thought & Emotion"

"Clear Communication"

"Handling Humanity"

"Free Your Spirit"

"Escaping Spirit-Traps"

"Eliminating Barriers"

"Conquest of Illusion"

All *sixteen* lesson-booklets of the newest
Professional Course on Mardukite Systemology
are combined together in *two volumes* as
"The Pathway to Ascension."

Lesson booklets are also available individually!

THE SYSTEMOL

Seekers and students of the *Basic Course* and *Professional Course* will also be interested in the *Systemology Core Research Series*. These eight volumes are a complete chronological record of the Mardukite New Thought developments from the Systemology Society, published in 2019 through 2023.

The *Systemology Core* begins with the first professional publication released when the *Mardukite Systemology Society* emerged from the underground in 2019, with: *"The Tablets of Destiny Revelation."*

OGY PATHWAY

The Tablets of Destiny Revelation:
*How Long-Lost Anunnaki Wisdom
Can Change the Fate of Humanity*

Crystal Clear: *Handbook for Seekers*

Metahuman Destinations (*2 volumes*)

Imaginomicon:
Approaching Gateways to Higher Universes

Way of the Wizard: *Utilitarian Systemology*

Systemology-180: *Fast-Track to Ascension*

Systemology Backtrack:
Reclaiming Spiritual Power & Past-Life Memory

PUBLISHED BY THE **JOSHUA FREE** IMPRINT REPRESENTING

The Mardukite Academy of Systemology

THE JOSHUA FREE IMPRINT
JFI PUBLICATIONS

MARDUKITE
ZUISM

mardukite.com

www.ingramcontent.com/pod-product-compliance
Lightning Source LLC
Chambersburg PA
CBHW071210120626
46546CB00006B/2499